My Math Rule Book

by Ingemar Anderson

First Edition, published 2024
Copyright© 2024 Ingemar Anderson

Cover Design and Interior Layout by Reprospace LLC, OpenAI DALL-E

Paperback ISBN-13: 978-1-952685-90-3

This book is designed with advice and directions from Viking Education Academy (www.viking-education.com), a K-12 tutoring and continuing education academy.

All rights reserved. No part of this book may be reproduced, stored in a retrieval system, or transmitted in any form or by any means—electronic, mechanical, photocopying, recording, or otherwise—without the prior written permission of the publisher, except in the case of brief quotations embodied in critical articles and reviews.

The contents of this book are intended for educational purposes only. The authors and contributors have made every effort to ensure the accuracy and completeness of the information presented. However, Viking Education Academy and the creators of this book assume no responsibility for errors, omissions, or any consequences arising from the use of this material.

For permissions and inquiries, contact:

Viking Education Academy
info@viking-education.com

KITSAP
PUBLISHING

Published by Kitsap Publishing
Poulsbo, WA 98370
www.KitsapPublishing.com

Introduction

WELCOME TO *MY RULE BOOK*!

This book is your personal space to capture all the math rules, formulas, and concepts you learn throughout your middle and high school years. By writing down what you've learned in your own words, you'll deepen your understanding and create a personalized study guide that you can refer back to anytime.

WHY MAKE YOUR OWN RULE BOOK?

Creating your own rule book helps you actively engage with the material, making it easier to remember and understand complex ideas. Research supports that writing down concepts in your own words significantly enhances memory retention and comprehension.

WHAT THE RESEARCH SAYS

- **Better Memory Through Self-Generation:** The Generation Effect shows that when people generate their own materials, rather than just passively receiving information, it leads to better memory retention and understanding (Slamecka & Graf, 1978). This means creating your own math rule book will help you remember formulas more effectively.

- **Handwriting vs. Typing:** A study by Mueller & Oppenheimer (2014) found that students who took notes by hand retained more information and had a deeper understanding of concepts compared to those who typed. Handwriting engages different parts of the brain, making information more meaningful and easier to recall.

- **Encoding and Memory:** Writing things down is a form of active learning known as "encoding." Research shows that encoding information deeply helps transfer it from short-term to long-term memory (*Craik & Lockhart, 1972*), making your personalized notes a powerful study tool.

- **Visual and Verbal Learning:** According to *Paivio's Dual Coding Theory (1971)*, combining text with visual elements (like diagrams or sketches) enhances learning by using both verbal and visual memory pathways. Adding your own drawings and examples to your math rule book will reinforce these connections.

Benefits:

- **Better Memory:** Writing rules in your own style makes the content stick longer.

- **Clarity and Confidence:** When you create your own definitions and solve problems, complex ideas become clearer.

- **Quick Review:** As your personalized reference guide, it's perfect for last-minute reviews before exams.

- Make "My Math Rule Book" your go-to resource for quick reference, confident learning, and success in math!

How to Use This Book

Record New Concepts: Whenever you learn a new rule or formula, jot it down here along with an example or two.

- **Organize by Topic:** The book is divided into sections like Algebra, Geometry, and Trigonometry to help you keep your notes organized.

- **Personalize It:** Feel free to add diagrams, doodles, or use colored pens—make it as unique as you are!

- **Review Regularly:** Periodically go back and review your entries to reinforce your memory. Also, use your rule book to look up rules while practicing math and for your homework.

Why Mathematics is All About Rules

Mathematics is often seen as the universal language of logic and reason, and at its core, it is governed by a set of well-defined rules. These rules are the building blocks that make mathematical thinking possible, allowing us to solve problems consistently and accurately.

The Foundation of Mathematical Rules

Consistency and Reliability: Mathematical rules ensure that calculations and problem-solving methods yield the same results every time, no matter who is performing them.

- **Building Complex Structures:** Simple rules can be combined to understand more complex concepts. For example, basic arithmetic leads to algebra, which in turn leads to calculus.

- **Universal Language:** Because mathematical rules are consistent worldwide, they allow people from different cultures and languages to communicate complex ideas without misunderstanding.

THE ROLE OF RULES IN PROBLEM-SOLVING

Guidance: Rules provide a roadmap for solving problems, telling us which steps to take and in what order.

- **Efficiency:** Knowing the appropriate rules helps us solve problems more quickly and with less effort.
- **Accuracy:** Adhering to mathematical rules minimizes errors, ensuring that our solutions are correct.

MATHEMATICS AS A RULE-BASED SYSTEM

Logical Framework: Mathematics relies on logic, and logic is governed by rules. These rules help us make valid inferences and draw correct conclusions.

Proof and Verification: Mathematical proofs are based on applying rules to verify that statements are universally true.

Predictability: Rules allow us to predict outcomes, which is essential in fields like physics, engineering, and economics.

EMBRACING THE RULES

Understanding that mathematics is all about rules empowers you to:

- **Master the Basics:** Grasp fundamental concepts that are crucial for more advanced topics.
- **Solve Real-World Problems:** Apply mathematical rules to find solutions in various fields like science, technology, and finance.
- **Develop Logical Thinking:** Enhance your ability to think critically and logically in everyday situations.

By recognizing that mathematics is built upon rules and embracing them fully, you lay a solid foundation for all your mathematical endeavors. Use this rule book to record, understand, and internalize these essential rules, making it an invaluable resource on your journey through mathematics.

Steps to Personalize Your Rule Book

Review Your Math Topics: Go through your class notes, textbooks, and any assignments to identify the key rules and concepts you've learned so far.

Customize the Table of Contents:

Add New Sections: If there are topics not listed in the current Table of Contents, feel free to add them.

Rearrange Sections: Organize the sections in a way that makes the most sense to you.

Number the Pages: As you fill in the content for each section, make sure to number your pages. Update the page numbers in your Table of Contents accordingly.

Create Clear Headings: For each rule or concept, write a clear and descriptive heading. This will make it easier to find specific information when you need to review.

Include Subtopics: Under main sections, list subtopics or specific rules. For example, under Fractions, you might include:

- Simplifying Fractions
- Adding and Subtracting Fractions
- Multiplying and Dividing Fractions
- Use Indexing Tabs or Colors

Why This Helps

Easy Reference: A well-organized Table of Contents allows you to find information quickly, saving you time during homework or exam prep.

Personalized Learning: Tailoring the content to your learning style makes the material more relatable and easier to understand.

Active Engagement: Writing and organizing the information yourself enhances memory retention.

Get Started!

Grab Your Writing Tools: Pens, pencils, highlighters—anything you like to use. Set Aside Some Time: Dedicate a quiet hour to focus on setting up your rule book.

Dive In: Begin filling in the Table of Contents and then proceed to the respective sections to jot down the rules, formulas, and examples.

Remember, this rule book is a reflection of your mathematical journey. The effort you put into organizing and personalizing it now will make it an invaluable resource in the future. Happy studying!

"My Math Rule Book" is a personalized guide designed by students, for students. This isn't your typical textbook—it's your tool for mastering math. With each page, you create your own collection of important formulas, key concepts, and essential rules in a way that makes sense to you.

Have fun!

My Table of Contents

Page #

Algebra

Fractions ....
Linear Equations ....
Quadratic Equations ....
Polynomials ....
Exponents and Radicals ....

Geometry

Angles and Lines ....
Triangles ....
Circles ....
Area and Volume ....

Trigonometry

Sine, Cosine, Tangent ....
Trigonometric Identities ....

Calculus

Limits ....
Derivatives ....
Integrals ....

Statistics and Probability

Mean, Median, Mode ....
Probability Rules ....

Additional Notes

Number Theory ....
Logic and Proofs ....
Miscellaneous Concepts ....

Additional Notes

....
....

Examples 149

National Pride: Gymnastics is a source of national pride in many countries, especially during the Olympics.

Physical Therapy: Many gymnasts use physical therapy as part of their training and recovery.

Gravity-Defying Feat: Gymnastics is often about defying gravity through jumps and flips.

Rhythmic Gymnastics: Rhythmic gymnastics, involving ribbons and hoops, was added to the Olympics in 1984.

Did you know gymnastics floors have springs and foam underneath? This helps gymnasts bounce higher and land safely, making those cool flips and jumps easier and safer!

Examples

EXPONENTS AND RADICALS

Laws of Exponents

1. **Product of Powers Rule**

    When multiplying two expressions with the same base, **add** the exponents.

    $$a^m \times a^n = a^{m+n}$$

    Example:

    $$2^3 \times 2^4 = 2^{3+4} = 2^7 = 128$$

2. **Quotient of Powers Rule**

    When dividing two expressions with the same base, **subtract** the exponents.

    $$\frac{a^m}{a^n} = a^{m-n}$$

    Example:

    $$\frac{5^5}{5^2} = 5^{5-2} = 5^3 = 125$$

3. **Power of a Power Rule**

    When raising a power to another power, **multiply** the exponents.

    $$(a^m)^n = a^{m \times n}$$

    Example:

    $$(3^2)^3 = 3^{2 \times 3} = 3^6 = 729$$

4. **Zero Exponent Rule**

   Any nonzero number raised to the zero power equals 1.

   $$a^0 = 1 \quad (\text{where } a \neq 0)$$

   Example:

   $$7^0 = 1$$

5. **Negative Exponent Rule**

   A negative exponent indicates the **reciprocal** of the base raised to the positive exponent.

   $$a^{-n} = \frac{1}{a^n} \quad (\text{where } a \neq 0)$$

   Example:

   $$2^{-3} = \frac{1}{2^3} = \frac{1}{8}$$

6. **Power of a Product Rule**

   When raising a product to a power, raise **each factor** to the power.

   $$(ab)^n = a^n b^n$$

   Example:

   $$(2 \times 5)^3 = 2^3 \times 5^3 = 8 \times 125 = 1,000$$

7. **Power of a Quotient Rule**

   When raising a quotient to a power, raise both the **numerator and the denominator** to the power.

   $$\left(\frac{a}{b}\right)^n = \frac{a^n}{b^n}$$

   Example:

   $$\left(\frac{3}{4}\right)^2 = \frac{3^2}{4^2} = \frac{9}{16}$$

Radicals (Roots)

1. **Definition of a Radical**

   The nth root of a number a is a number that, when raised to the nth power, equals a.

   $$\sqrt[n]{a} = a^{1/n}$$

   Example:

   $$\sqrt[3]{8} = 8^{1/3} = 2$$

2. **Simplifying Square Roots**

   Factor the number under the square root into its prime factors and extract pairs.

   Example:

   $$\sqrt{18} = \sqrt{9 \times 2} = \sqrt{9} \times \sqrt{2} = 3\sqrt{2}$$

3. **Multiplying Radicals**

   Multiply the numbers under the radicals and keep them under a single radical sign.

   $$\sqrt{a} \times \sqrt{b} = \sqrt{a \times b}$$

   Example:

   $$\sqrt{2} \times \sqrt{3} = \sqrt{2 \times 3} = \sqrt{6}$$

4. Dividing Radicals

Divide the numbers under the radicals and keep them under a single radical sign.

$$\frac{\sqrt{a}}{\sqrt{b}} = \sqrt{\frac{a}{b}}$$

Example:

$$\frac{\sqrt{8}}{\sqrt{2}} = \sqrt{\frac{8}{2}} = \sqrt{4} = 2$$

5. Rational Exponents

Radicals can be expressed using fractional exponents.

$$a^{m/n} = \sqrt[n]{a^m} = \left(\sqrt[n]{a}\right)^m$$

Example:

$$16^{3/2} = \left(\sqrt{16}\right)^3 = 4^3 = 64$$

Important Notes

- Combining Exponents and Radicals

  Understanding that exponents and radicals are interconnected helps in simplifying complex expressions.

- Rationalizing the Denominator

  Eliminate radicals from the denominator by multiplying the numerator and denominator by an appropriate radical.

  Example:

  $$\frac{1}{\sqrt{5}} = \frac{\sqrt{5}}{\sqrt{5} \times \sqrt{5}} = \frac{\sqrt{5}}{5}$$

- Solving Radical Equations

  To solve equations with radicals, isolate the radical and then raise both sides of the equation to eliminate the radical.

  Example:

  Solve for x:

  $$\sqrt{x+3} = 5$$
  $$x + 3 = 25$$
  $$x = 22$$

Questions

1. Simplify the expression:

$$2^5 \times 2^3$$

2. Simplify the expression:

$$\frac{9^4}{9^2}$$

3. Simplify the expression:

$$(5^2)^3$$

4. Evaluate the expression:

$$81^{1/2}$$

5. Simplify the expression with a negative exponent:

$$4^{-1}$$

6. Write the expression with positive exponents and simplify:

$$\left(\frac{2}{3}\right)^{-2}$$

7. Simplify the radical expression:

$$\sqrt{72}$$

8. Simplify the product of radicals:

$$\sqrt{5} \times \sqrt{20}$$

Extra Challenge

Solve for x:

$$\sqrt{x+5} = 4$$

Tips for Success

- Remember the **laws of exponents** when simplifying expressions.
- For radicals, look for perfect squares (or cubes) that can be factored out.
- When rationalizing denominators, multiply the numerator and denominator by the radical in the denominator.
- Convert between radical expressions and expressions with rational exponents when it makes simplification easier.

Step-by-Step Solution

Step 1: Isolate the Radical (It's already isolated)

The square root is already isolated on one side of the equation.

Step 2: Square Both Sides to Eliminate the Square Root

To remove the square root, square both sides of the equation:

$$\left(\sqrt{x+5}\right)^2 = 4^2$$

This simplifies to:

$$x + 5 = 16$$

Step 3: Solve for x

Subtract 5 from both sides to isolate x:

$$x + 5 - 5 = 16 - 5$$

Simplify:

$$x = 11$$

Step 4: Check for Extraneous Solutions

When dealing with square roots, it's important to check the solution in the original equation to ensure it's valid.

Substitute $x = 11$ back into the original equation:

$$\sqrt{11 + 5} = \sqrt{16} = 4$$

Since the left-hand side equals the right-hand side:

$$4 = 4$$

The solution $x = 11$ is valid.

Explanation

- **Why Square Both Sides?** Squaring both sides eliminates the square root, allowing us to solve for x using basic algebra.
- **Checking the Solution:** Squaring both sides can sometimes introduce extraneous solutions. Substituting back into the original equation ensures the solution is valid.

Final Thoughts

Great job solving the equation! Remember, whenever you have an equation involving a square root:

1. **Isolate the radical** if it's not already isolated.
2. **Square both sides** to eliminate the radical.
3. **Solve the resulting equation** for the variable.
4. **Check your solution** in the original equation to verify its validity.

www.ingramcontent.com/pod-product-compliance
Lightning Source LLC
Chambersburg PA
CBHW060526080526
44586CB00012B/636